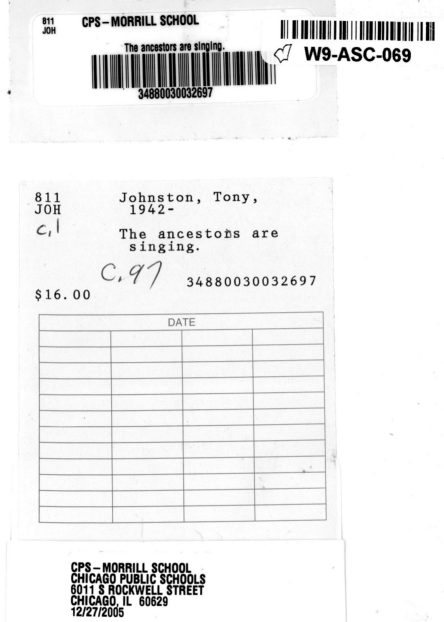

811
JOH
c.1

Johnston, Tony,
  1942-

The ancestors are
singing.

C.97   34880030032697

$16.00

DATE			

The Ancestors Are Singing

The Ancestors Are Singing

TONY JOHNSTON

Pictures by KAREN BARBOUR

Farrar Straus Giroux / New York

For my *queridos* Rhoads and Sorsbys.
Como ellos no hay más.

T.J.

Text copyright © 2003 by the Johnston Family Trust
Illustrations copyright © 2003 by Karen Barbour
All rights reserved
Distributed in Canada by Douglas & McIntyre Ltd.
Printed in the United States of America
Designed by Nancy Goldenberg
First edition, 2003
10 9 8 7 6 5 4 3 2 1

Library of Congress Cataloging-in-Publication Data
Johnston, Tony.
    The ancestors are singing / Tony Johnston ; pictures by Karen Barbour.
        p.   cm.
    Summary: A collection of poems reflecting the culture, customs, daily life,
and history of Mexico.
        ISBN 0-374-30347-9
        1. Mexico—Juvenile poetry.   2. Children's poetry, American.   [1. Mexico—
Poetry.   2. American poetry.]   I. Barbour, Karen, ill.   II. Title.

PS3560.0393 A84 2003
811'.54—dc21
                                                                    2002020704

Como México no hay dos.
Like Mexico there is no other.

Contents

The Ancestors Are Singing

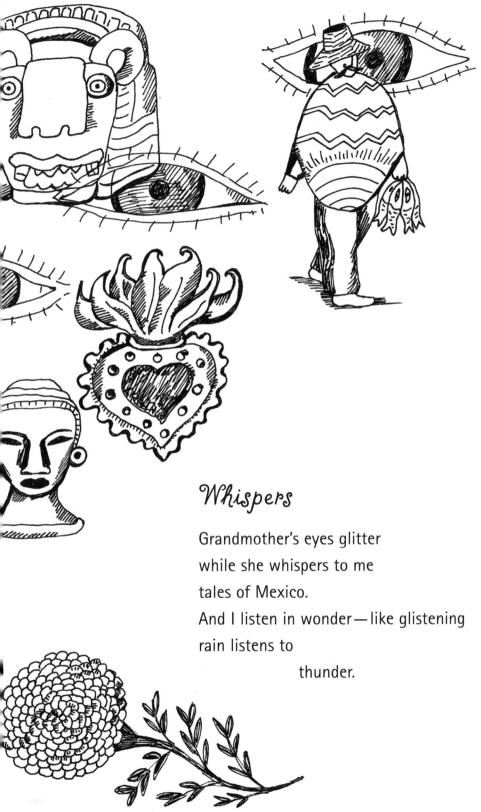

Whispers

Grandmother's eyes glitter
while she whispers to me
tales of Mexico.
And I listen in wonder—like glistening
rain listens to
              thunder.

Old Powers

The day some people trucked
the colossal Tláloc
from his forever-home
to adorn a museum,
the disgruntled god
loosed a flood
and those who had
forgotten that Old One
believed again.

Storms in Oaxaca

The great saguaro shivers
in the cold.
It holds out its thick and prickly arms
to feel slivers of shining
rain.
Tall and alone it stands
and gathers light from strikes of raving
lightning.
When the land is dry, the saguaro remembers
storms.

Rainy Season, Mexico City

Now begins a thin tin rain
on all the cars
downtown.

Now it pours as if from jars,
ollas,
upside down.

Now it beats in shining sheets.
Every horn
sounds.

Can this silver skein of cars
ever
be unwound?

Seekers

They came from Aztlán,
land of herons,
walking in sandaled
                    feet
stirring up
        dust
seeking a place.

Like the *shirrr* of a desert snake
their name chilled the
                        bones
of all they met
for they were deadly
fierce.

They have vanished. Like dust.

But they still *shirrr*
down the paths of our minds—
                Chichimecas.

Dust Devils

Like shimmering spirits they come
spiraling
over trees
spinning
under donkeys
anywhere they please
they twist
they leap
lifting the tops
off dusty roads
taking them
to my house
for Mami
to sweep.

Grandmother's Grinding Stone

Grandmother's grinding stone knows
the secrets of her mother
and her mother
and *her* mother—
like leaves fluttering
on our family tree.
Someday it will reveal them
to me.

Quetzalcóatl

In the world's young days,
Quetzalcóatl, the Serpent, met Farmer
beside a rustling plant.

Like wind he whispered
in Farmer's ear,
This is my gift to you.
Its leaves are more precious
than quetzal plumes,
its heart richer than jade.
Farmer asked, "What is its name?"

And the Serpent whispered,
Maize.

Jalapeño Day

On a jalapeño day—hot, hot, hot—
I drift out my window
and over our earthen plot
where Papi trails the ox
behind a cloud of dust,
planting grains of maize.
From high above, I wave.
¡Hola! I shout, shout, shout.

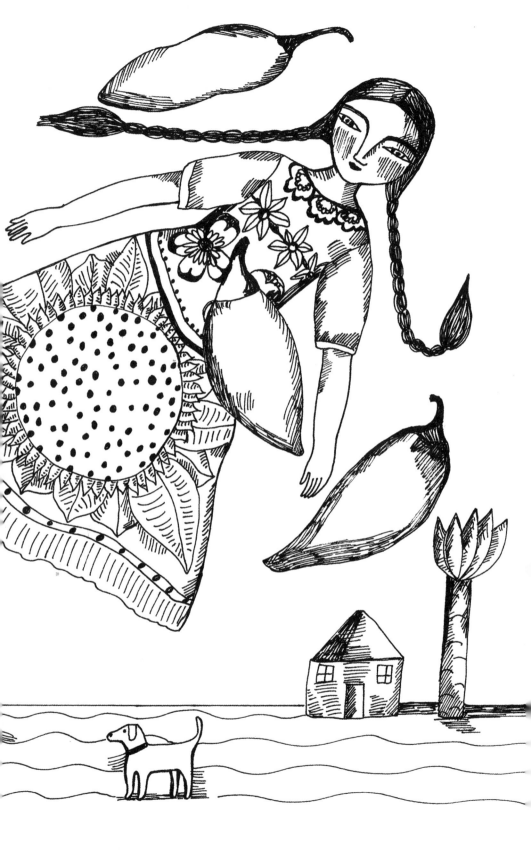

Obsidian

Slivers of blackness
shining in hot cornfields.
Did Ixta spit you out?

Anahuacalli

Diego, the painter, built a museum
for the People.
He built it of dark thick lava stone.
Lava stone from hot-bellied volcanoes.
Diego, the painter, filled its dark rooms
with ancient sculptures of clay and stone.
Ancient sculptures of gods and snakes
and little curled-up dogs and frogs
(because he looked like one)
for the People.
The painter, Diego, made an altar.
An altar piled with savory foods
and strewn with armloads of marigolds
for the People.
Through these musty rooms, now, Diego's ghost
floats and chuckles
and sifts down dust of astonishing colors
(like crushed rainbows).
Dust ground from his dried-out paints.
Dust that drifts onto the hats
and the shirtsleeves and the dresses and the shawls
and the broken shoes
of the People.

A Boy Named José

A boy named José
sells newspapers
on the corner
every day
at cold still-dark.
He has no shoes.
Every day I see him.
A boy named José
who has no shoes.

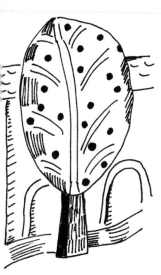

Chapultepec Park

Sundays in Chapultepec
people swarm and buzz like cheerful
bees
the gossip of the week
and dogs come to sniff
other dogs or anything else
that they happen upon
and birds peck at spilled popcorn
like puffs of tiny clouds
and an organ-grinder grinds out
happiness
in notes held inside a wooden box
while his monkey catches coins
in its little red hat—
pennies for happiness
and unruly children run in unruly
grass
and a fountain sings old songs
the water knows
and the best thing is the balloons—
bright moons the color of joy—
that tug and pull and strain
to float back to the sky.

Rabbit in the Moon

Old and clever one,
how I wish I had been there
on the night that you leaped
into the sky.
How I wish I had seen you spark
your silver trail
like a comet with long ears
across the dark.
Oh, how I wish I had been there—
and looked up.

Moon over Mexico

The moon's white eye
watches over skyscrapers
and stone temples alike.

Temple

A little snake
sleeping in a crack
of an old temple.

A little snake,
ribbon-thin,
so colorful a ripple.

Old Palaces

Beneath the jungle canopy of trees,
old palaces fill the silence with old dreams,
alone except when splendid golden gleams
of jaguars come to rest upon their bones—
or when bats, velvet gods of long ago,
cluster in their crumbling roof combs.
The ancient trees stand, green as quetzal plumes.
The fearsome kings are gone. Stones speak to stones.

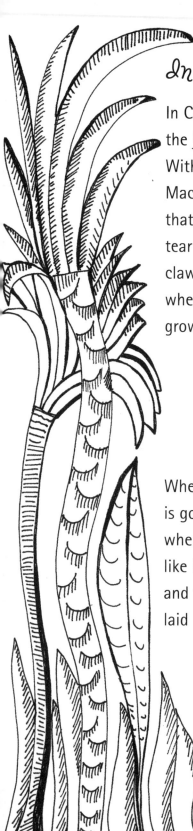

In Chiapas

In Chiapas they are cutting
the jungle down.
With machetes. Saws.
Machines
that screech, whine,
tear the vines,
claw
where sacred *ceibas*
grow.

     Where will the monkeys,
     the jaguars
     go?

When the green
is gone,
when trees are strewn
like bones
and the ancient *ceibas*
laid low,

     Where will the monkeys,
     the jaguars
     go?

In Veracruz There Is a Bay

In Veracruz there is a bay
Sun-polished as turquoise.
There came sailing in one day
A man—Hernán Cortés.
Nothing since he passed that way
Stayed ever as it was
In all that world of yesterday
Except the sky above.

Church of Santa María Tonantzintla

"Build my church," the Spaniard said
his voice grim
as the grave.

The Indian did.
He had no choice.
He was a slave.

He built it strong. He built it thick.
With his life
he built the place.

But he gave each saint and angel there
his own dark
Indian face.

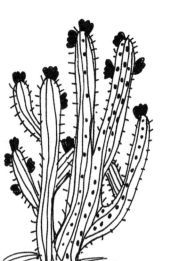

Indian's Lament

For time out of mind
the People wore clothing
of colors rainbow-bright.

The Spaniards.
They made us wear
white.

Small Church

Each Sunday the little boy,
in his best suit, gazes
out the window and dreams.
He wishes to own a suit
of cloud.
He hopes to eat a green
balloon (like a green-skinned melon),
to spit out seeds that will become
green balloon-trees.
He longs to trill shrill songs
with crickets.
The little boy dreams wide dreams.
While everyone closely watches the padre,
the little boy, never
touching the ground, rides a swift
blue horse.

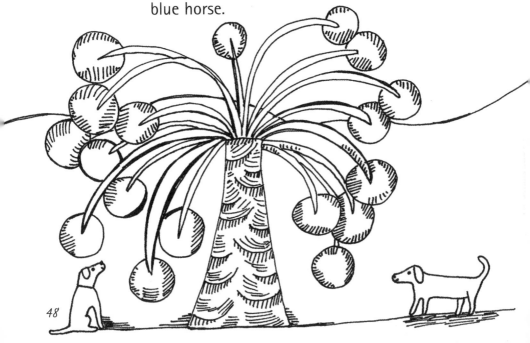

Near the Zócalo

I saw the place
where the Old Ones
received the sign—
of eagle, serpent, *nopal*.
Then they were wanderers
no more.

I stood there.
I stood there.

Quetzalcóatl Lies Sleeping

Quetzalcóatl lies sleeping
in the tall green corn.
His plumes shake
in wind
like thin long leaves.
Quetzalcóatl lies dreaming
in the tall green corn.
When
will he awake?

Texcoco

The lake is gone
where Tenochtitlán rose.
Listen—
the song of old waters.

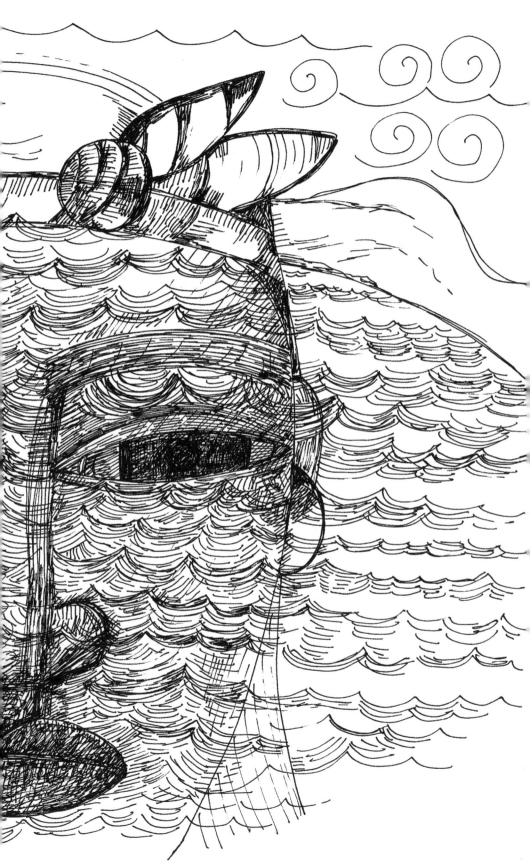

Once an Aztec Had a Flute

Once an Aztec had a flute of clay
gouged from the banks
of a river.
When he played, out poured notes
　　　　　　　　like water.

I have a flute of cinnamon bark,
a perfumed curl of *canela*
good and brown.
When I play, out floats my song
　　　　　　　of cinnamon.

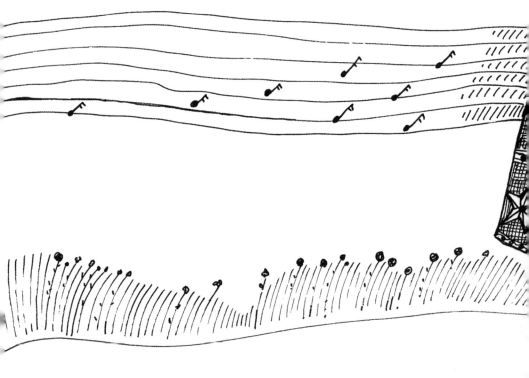

Calaca, Day of the Dead

The *tlak-tlak* of bones—
a skeleton, dancing loosely
with the wind.

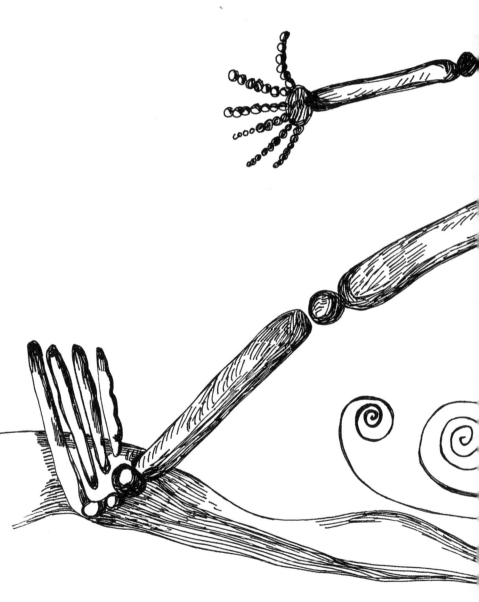

Posada, Tepotzotlán

Come to the courtyard at evening.
Stroll the path lined with candles
in tin holders.
Sip sweet punch, cinnamon-strong,
while cinnamon-songs rise
to please the ears
of the moon,
while night spills
through myriad old
stars.
Stilled with wonder, watch bold
San Miguel
rush through flames of poinsettias
to vanquish the splendid
red Devil.

Museum of Anthropology
(for Pedro Ramírez Vázquez)

In the silence of the splendid galleries
Ehécatl, god of wind,
stands forever entwined
with a slender snake.
Alongside a mute clay
flute,
a wooden Aztec drum
rests, stilled
as if it had never
beat.
Mezcala figurines
carved in green stone
sit gazing at old stars beyond
the ceiling.

In the courtyard
beneath a stone pillar
streaming
with musical water,
the Ancestors are
singing.

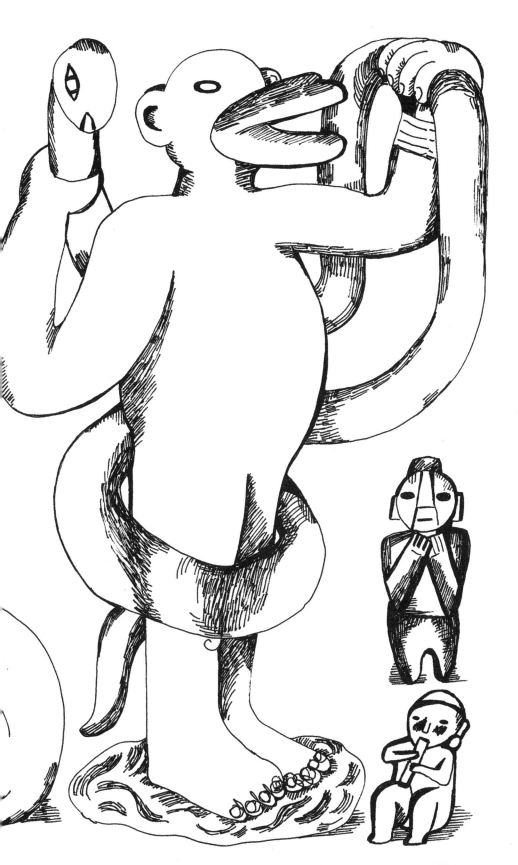

Glossary

Anahuacalli (*ah-nah-wah-KAH-lee*): the museum built by Diego Rivera to house his pre-Columbian antiquities for the Mexican people.

Aztec (*AZ-tek*): an ancient tribe of Mexico.

Aztlán (*az-TLAHN*): the mythological homeland of the Aztecs.

calaca (*kah-LAH-kah*): skeleton.

canela (*kah-NAY-lah*): cinnamon.

ceiba (*SAY-ee-bah*): the sacred tree of the Maya.

Chapultepec Park (*cha-pool-teh-PEK*): a large park in Mexico City. The Museum of Anthropology is located there.

Chiapas (*chee-AH-pahs*): Mexican state; part of the Maya homeland.

Chichimecas (*chee-chee-MAY-kahs*): ancient barbarian tribes of Mexico from which came, among others, the Mexica, or Aztecs.

Diego (*dee-AY-go*): Diego Rivera, a Mexican painter.

Ehécatl (*ay-HAY-kah-tul*): the Aztec god of wind.

Hernán Cortés (*air-NAHN kor-TAYS*): the leader of the Spanish invasion of Mexico, which began in 1519.

hola (*OH-la*): hello.

Ixta (*ICKS-tah*): the volcano Ixtaccíhuatl (*ICKS-tah-SEE-wah-tul*); a sleeping princess, according to Mexican legend.

jalapeño (*hal-lah-PAIN-yo*): a kind of chili pepper.

Mami (*MAH-mee*): Mommy.

Maya (*MY-ya*): an ancient tribe of Mexico, isolated groups of which still exist.

Mezcala (*mez-CAH-la*): an ancient culture from the Mexican state of Guerrero.

nopal (*noh-PAHL*): prickly pear cactus.

Oaxaca (*wah-HAH-kah*): Mexican state; also its capital.

olla (*OY-yah*): jar.

Papi (*PAH-pee*): Daddy.

posada (*poh-SAH-dah*): the Mexican Christmas celebration in which Mary and Joseph's search to find lodging is reenacted.

quetzal (*kett-ZAL*): a bird, now nearly extinct, found mainly in Mexico and Guatemala; the quetzal was so prized by the ancient Aztecs that the penalty for harming one was death.

Quetzalcóatl (*kett-zal-KOH-ah-tul*): the plumed serpent god of Mexican mythology. According to myth, he gave corn to man and in a Second Coming will appear to save the Mexican people.

San Miguel (*san mee-GELL*): Saint Michael the archangel.

Santa María Tonantzintla (*SAHN-tah mah-REE-ah toh-nahnt-ZEENT-la*): a Spanish colonial church in the Mexican state of Puebla.

Tenochtitlán (*teh-noch-tit-LAHN*): the ancient capital of the Aztecs; the Spaniards built Mexico City over the site.

Tepotzotlán (*teh-poht-zoht-LAHN*): a Spanish colonial church near Mexico City; the story of Saint Michael vanquishing the devil is reenacted there each Christmas.

Tezcoco (*tez-KOH-koh*): the lake, almost dry, upon which the Aztecs built their capital, Tenochtitlán.

Tláloc (*TLAH-lohk*): the Aztec god of rain.

Veracruz (*vay-rah-KROOZ*): Mexican state, also its capital; a nearby bay is the site where the ships of the Spanish conquerors first landed in Mexico.

Zócalo (*ZOH-kah-loh*): the main square, or La Plaza de la Constitución, in downtown Mexico City.